The Memory Catcher

An Interactive Journal
That Uncovers Forgotten
Memories From Your Past

Veronica Slater & Jessica Fletcher

ISBN: 978-1-953596-04-8 (paperback)
ISBN: 978-1-953596-05-5 (hardback)

First Edition, 2020
The Publishing Portal
Los Angeles, California
www.thepublishingportal.com

Printed in United States of America

Dedication

Grandpa Ralph, the memories you've shared
have strengthened our bond and my hope is that this
journal can be a way to strengthen connections
across generations just as it has for you and I.

Acknowledgements

We want to take the opportunity to share how grateful
we are to all of our collaborators on this project.

The completion of this project would not have been possible
without the help of several integral individuals. A special thank
you to Sonale for believing in this journal from the beginning
and helping us put our idea on paper. You took our abstract
idea and put it into a concrete format that illustrated our vision.
We also want to thank Tisha Morris for helping us through the
process of publishing our first journal. It has been an incredible
learning experience and we are so grateful to have had you
both throughout our Memory Catcher journey.

About the Authors

Veronica Slater & Jessica Fletcher have a passion for helping individuals through their journey of self-growth in their professional and personal lives. As young sales professionals, they have learned the power of asking the right questions to develop deeper connections with those in their network. Their diverse experiences have reinforced their belief that life is full of memorable moments and life lessons. The goal of this publication is to provide them with the tools necessary for self-reflection, memory retention, and generational story sharing. Veronica and Jessica have chosen to give back 5% of the proceeds to Alzheimer nonprofits.

How to Use The Memory Catcher

No matter what your age or where you are in your life's journey, you have certain events that you remember and others you have forgotten...or so you think. This journal is designed to dive deeper into your subconscious where you hold all of your most precious life experiences by feeding you prompts that help you uncover forgotten moments in time. These memories that you are capturing in this journal are not only meant for self-reflection but also aim to help future and past generations understand how your experiences have shaped you into the individual you are today. Your vulnerability within a certain life experience may comfort others through a similar struggle or inspire future generations to pursue their dreams. **The bad and the good have a place in this journal because both have contributed to your identity so make sure to include both in your narrative.**

Here are some key ideas to keep in mind when illustrating your story:

- The keywords are prompts, but they cannot describe your feelings during and after the moment has passed. **Be mindful that your feeling in the moment of the memory may be different than your feeling in the present.**

- Sometimes the first memory that comes to mind may not be the most impactful. Try and **think of a few different memories with that keyword and then identify the most significant story to tell.**

- There are many memories associated with what went wrong in our lives. These do not have to be negative. **How can you write the narrative in a way that highlights the lesson learned from that experience?**

This journal is designed to help you retain all the key elements of your story, which is why we offer an outline template on the left side of each page to help organize the details of your memory. The Context Clues on the right side of each page are there to highlight important aspects of the memory in order to efficiently capture the whole picture.

We hope that this journal helps you to develop a new perspective about the past, and that it provides you with a deeper understanding and appreciation for both the bad and good experiences in your life.

We would love to hear about your experience and read your stories if you are willing to share. :)

Contact us at @memorycatcherjournal and tag us on Instagram or Facebook for a feature on our page of your memory catcher journey.

Memory Joggers

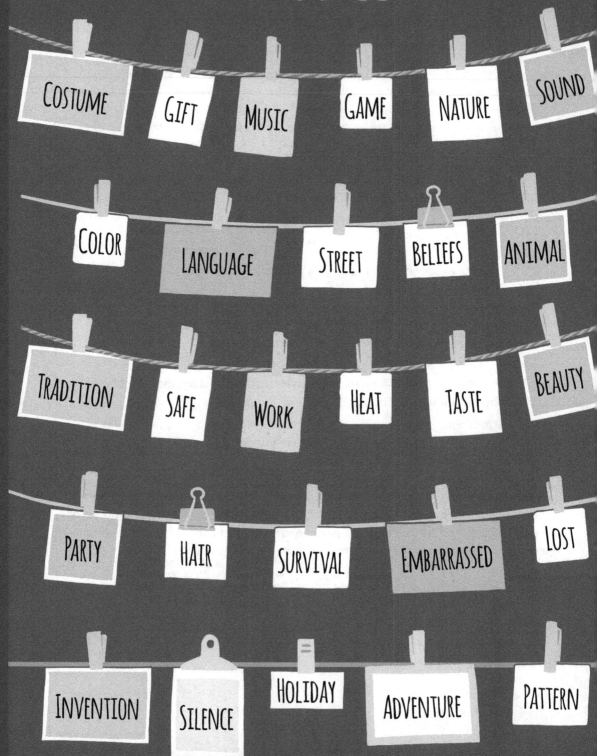

COSTUME · GIFT · MUSIC · GAME · NATURE · SOUND

COLOR · LANGUAGE · STREET · BELIEFS · ANIMAL

TRADITION · SAFE · WORK · HEAT · TASTE · BEAUTY

PARTY · HAIR · SURVIVAL · EMBARRASSED · LOST

INVENTION · SILENCE · HOLIDAY · ADVENTURE · PATTERN

Memory Joggers

FRIENDSHIP · SCHOOL · MONEY · CITY · MIDDLE · SURPRISE

CRISIS · TRANSPORTATION · FREEDOM · WATER · CANDY

COMPETITION · CRUSH · SLEEP · SEAT · SECRET · RANDOM

TOOL · SUPPORTED · PUBERTY · MOVIE · SEASON

GREETING · SHOES · TEAM · COMMUNITY · NUMBER

**Life Stage:** _____ **Place:** _____
(Child, Teen, Adult, etc.)

Characters:

Memory Box:
(Insert photo or draw image that connects to memory)

Why are you grateful for this story?
(lesson learned, how you felt, long term impact)

_____
_____
_____
_____
_____
_____
_____
_____

(Insert word here)

Context Clues

1) _____
2) _____
3) _____

(Name your story)

Life Stage: _____   **Place:** _____
(Child, Teen, Adult, etc.)

Characters:

Memory Box:
(Insert photo or draw image that connects to memory)

Why are you grateful for this story?
(lesson learned, how you felt, long term impact)

_____

_____

_____

_____

_____

_____

_____

_____

(Insert word here)

Context Clues

1) _____
2) _____
3) _____

_____
(Name your story)

**Start** **Life Stage:** _____ **Place:** _____

(Child, Teen, Adult, etc.)

Characters:

Memory Box:
(Insert photo or draw image that connects to memory)

Why are you grateful for this story?
(lesson learned, how you felt, long term impact)

_____

_____

_____

_____

_____

_____

_____

_____

(Insert word here)

Context Clues

1) _____

2) _____

3) _____

(Name your story)

Life Stage: _____   **Place:** _____
(Child, Teen, Adult, etc.)

Characters:

Memory Box:
(Insert photo or draw image that connects to memory)

Why are you grateful for this story?
(lesson learned, how you felt, long term impact)

_____

_____

_____

_____

_____

_____

_____

Context Clues

1) _____

2) _____

3) _____

_____
(Name your story)

Life Stage: _____

(Child, Teen, Adult, etc.)

Place: _____

Characters:

Memory Box:

(Insert photo or draw image that connects to memory)

Why are you grateful for this story?

(lesson learned, how you felt, long term impact)

_____

_____

_____

_____

_____

_____

_____

(Insert word here)

Context Clues

1) _____

2) _____

3) _____

_____
(Name your story)

Life Stage: _____   **Place:** _____
(Child, Teen, Adult, etc.)

Characters:

Memory Box:
(Insert photo or draw image that connects to memory)

Why are you grateful for this story?
(lesson learned, how you felt, long term impact)

_____

_____

_____

_____

_____

_____

_____

_____

Context Clues

1) _____

2) _____

3) _____

(Insert word here)

_____
(Name your story)

 **Life Stage:** _____   **Place:** _____

(Child, Teen, Adult, etc.)

Characters:

Memory Box:
(Insert photo or draw image that connects to memory)

Why are you grateful for this story?
(lesson learned, how you felt, long term impact)

_____

_____

_____

_____

_____

_____

_____

(Insert word here)

Context Clues

1) _____
2) _____
3) _____

(Name your story)

_____

_____

_____

_____

_____

_____

_____

_____

_____

_____

_____

_____

_____

_____

_____

_____

_____

Life Stage: _____   **Place:** _____
(Child, Teen, Adult, etc.)

Characters:

Memory Box:
(Insert photo or draw image that connects to memory)

Why are you grateful for this story?
(lesson learned, how you felt, long term impact)

_____
_____
_____
_____
_____
_____
_____
_____

Context Clues

1) _____

2) _____

3) _____

_____
(Insert word here)

_____
(Name your story)

Life Stage: _____

(Child, Teen, Adult, etc.)

Place: _____

Characters:

Memory Box:
(Insert photo or draw image that connects to memory)

Why are you grateful for this story?
(lesson learned, how you felt, long term impact)

_____

_____

_____

_____

_____

_____

_____

_____

(Insert word here)

Context Clues

1) _____

2) _____

3) _____

(Name your story)

Life Stage: _____   **Place:** _____
(Child, Teen, Adult, etc.)

Characters:

Memory Box:
(Insert photo or draw image that connects to memory)

Why are you grateful for this story?
(lesson learned, how you felt, long term impact)

_____

_____

_____

_____

_____

_____

_____

_____

(Insert word here)

Context Clues

1) _____

2) _____

3) _____

_____
(Name your story)

Life Stage: _____
(Child, Teen, Adult, etc.)

Place: _____

Characters:

Memory Box:
(Insert photo or draw image that connects to memory)

Why are you grateful for this story?
(lesson learned, how you felt, long term impact)

(Insert word here)

Context Clues

1) _____

2) _____

3) _____

_____
(Name your story)

Life Stage: _____

(Child, Teen, Adult, etc.)

Place: _____

Characters:

Memory Box:

(Insert photo or draw image that connects to memory)

Why are you grateful for this story?

(lesson learned, how you felt, long term impact)

_____

_____

_____

_____

_____

_____

_____

_____

_____

Context Clues

(Insert word here)

1) _____

2) _____

3) _____

_____

(Name your story)

 **Life Stage:** _____ **Place:** _____
(Child, Teen, Adult, etc.)

Characters:

Memory Box:
(Insert photo or draw image that connects to memory)

Why are you grateful for this story?
(lesson learned, how you felt, long term impact)

_____
_____
_____
_____
_____
_____
_____
_____

(Insert word here)

Context Clues

1) _____

2) _____

3) _____

(Name your story)

Start

Life Stage: _____
(Child, Teen, Adult, etc.)

Place: _____

Characters:

Memory Box:
(Insert photo or draw image that connects to memory) .

Why are you grateful for this story?
(lesson learned, how you felt, long term impact)

Context Clues

1) _____
2) _____
3) _____

(Insert word here)

_____
(Name your story)

Life Stage: _____ **Place:** _____
(Child, Teen, Adult, etc.)

Characters:

Memory Box:
(Insert photo or draw image that connects to memory)

Why are you grateful for this story?
(lesson learned, how you felt, long term impact)

_____

_____

_____

_____

_____

_____

_____

(Insert word here)

Context Clues

1) _____

2) _____

3) _____

_____
(Name your story)

Life Stage: _____
(Child, Teen, Adult, etc.)

Place: _____

Characters:

Memory Box:
(Insert photo or draw image that connects to memory)

Why are you grateful for this story?
(lesson learned, how you felt, long term impact)

_____

_____

_____

_____

_____

_____

_____

(Insert word here)

Context Clues

1) _____

2) _____

3) _____

_____
(Name your story)

Start **Life Stage:** _____ **Place:** _____
(Child, Teen, Adult, etc.)

Characters:

Memory Box:
(Insert photo or draw image that connects to memory)

Why are you grateful for this story?
(lesson learned, how you felt, long term impact)

(Insert word here)

Context Clues

1) _____

2) _____

3) _____

_____
(Name your story)

Life Stage: _____
(Child, Teen, Adult, etc.)

Place: _____

Characters:

Memory Box:
(Insert photo or draw image that connects to memory)

Why are you grateful for this story?
(lesson learned, how you felt, long term impact)

_____
_____
_____
_____
_____
_____
_____
_____

(Insert word here)

Context Clues

1) _____

2) _____

3) _____

_____
(Name your story)

Life Stage: _____ **Place:** _____

(Child, Teen, Adult, etc.)

Characters:

Memory Box:

(Insert photo or draw image that connects to memory)

Why are you grateful for this story?

(lesson learned, how you felt, long term impact)

_____

_____

_____

_____

_____

_____

_____

(Insert word here)

Context Clues

1) _____

2) _____

3) _____

_____
(Name your story)

 **Life Stage:** _____ **Place:** _____

(Child, Teen, Adult, etc.)

Characters:

Memory Box:

(Insert photo or draw image that connects to memory)

Why are you grateful for this story?

(lesson learned, how you felt, long term impact)

Context Clues

1) _____
2) _____
3) _____

(Insert word here)

_____
(Name your story)

Life Stage: _____ **Place:** _____
(Child, Teen, Adult, etc.)

Characters:

Memory Box:
(Insert photo or draw image that connects to memory)

Why are you grateful for this story?
(lesson learned, how you felt, long term impact)

_____

_____

_____

_____

_____

_____

_____

_____

(Insert word here)

Context Clues

1) _____
2) _____
3) _____

(Name your story)

Life Stage: _____ **Place:** _____
(Child, Teen, Adult, etc.)

Characters:

Memory Box:
(Insert photo or draw image that connects to memory)

Why are you grateful for this story?
(lesson learned, how you felt, long term impact)

_____

_____

_____

_____

_____

_____

_____

_____

Context Clues

_____

(Insert word here)

1) _____
2) _____
3) _____

_____
(Name your story)

 **Life Stage:** _____ **Place:** _____

(Child, Teen, Adult, etc.)

Characters:

Memory Box:

(Insert photo or draw image that connects to memory)

Why are you grateful for this story?

(lesson learned, how you felt, long term impact)

_____

_____

_____

_____

_____

_____

_____

(Insert word here)

Context Clues

1) ....

2) ....

3) ....

(Name your story)

Life Stage: _____ **Place:** _____

Characters:

Memory Box:

(Insert photo or draw image that connects to memory)

Why are you grateful for this story?

(lesson learned, how you felt, long term impact)

Context Clues

(Insert word here)

1) _____
2) _____
3) _____

_____
(Name your story)

_____
_____
_____
_____
_____
_____
_____
_____
_____
_____
_____
_____
_____
_____
_____
_____
_____
_____
_____
_____

Life Stage: _____   **Place:** _____
(Child, Teen, Adult, etc.)

Characters:

Memory Box:
(Insert photo or draw image that connects to memory)

Why are you grateful for this story?
(lesson learned, how you felt, long term impact)

_____

_____

_____

_____

_____

_____

_____

_____

_____

(Insert word here)

Context Clues

1) _____

2) _____

3) _____

_____
(Name your story)

Life Stage: _____ **Place:** _____

(Child, Teen, Adult, etc.)

Characters:

Memory Box:

(Insert photo or draw image that connects to memory)

Why are you grateful for this story?

(lesson learned, how you felt, long term impact)

_____

_____

_____

_____

_____

_____

_____

_____

(Insert word here)

Context Clues

1) _____

2) _____

3) _____

_____
(Name your story)

Life Stage: _____   **Place:** _____
(Child, Teen, Adult, etc.)

Characters:

Memory Box:
(Insert photo or draw image that connects to memory)

Why are you grateful for this story?
(lesson learned, how you felt, long term impact)

_____

_____

_____

_____

_____

_____

_____

(Insert word here)

Context Clues

1) ....

2) ....

3) ....

_____

(Name your story)

 **Life Stage:** _____ **Place:** _____
(Child, Teen, Adult, etc.)

Characters:

Memory Box:
(Insert photo or draw image that connects to memory)

Why are you grateful for this story?
(lesson learned, how you felt, long term impact)

_____
_____
_____
_____
_____
_____
_____
_____

(Insert word here)

Context Clues

1) _____

2) _____

3) _____

_____
(Name your story)

Life Stage: _____   **Place:** _____
(Child, Teen, Adult, etc.)

Characters:

Memory Box:
(Insert photo or draw image that connects to memory)

Why are you grateful for this story?
(lesson learned, how you felt, long term impact)

(Insert word here)

Context Clues

1) _____
2) _____
3) _____

(Name your story)

Life Stage: _____
<small>(Child, Teen, Adult, etc.)</small>

Place: _____

Characters:

Memory Box:
<small>(Insert photo or draw image that connects to memory)</small>

Why are you grateful for this story?
<small>(lesson learned, how you felt, long term impact)</small>

_____

_____

_____

_____

_____

_____

_____

Context Clues

1) _____
2) _____
3) _____

(Insert word here)

_____
(Name your story)

_____

_____

_____

_____

_____

_____

_____

_____

_____

_____

_____

_____

_____

_____

_____

_____

_____

_____

_____

_____

_____

Start

Life Stage: _____
(Child, Teen, Adult, etc.)

Place: _____

Characters:

Memory Box:
(Insert photo or draw image that connects to memory)

Why are you grateful for this story?
(lesson learned, how you felt, long term impact)

(Insert word here)

Context Clues

1) _____

2) _____

3) _____

_____
(Name your story)

Life Stage: _____
(Child, Teen, Adult, etc.)

Place: _____

Characters:

Memory Box:
(Insert photo or draw image that connects to memory)

Why are you grateful for this story?
(lesson learned, how you felt, long term impact)

_____

_____

_____

_____

_____

_____

_____

_____

Context Clues

(Insert word here)

1) _____
2) _____
3) _____

_____
(Name your story)

 **Life Stage:** _____ **Place:** _____
(Child, Teen, Adult, etc.)

Characters:

Memory Box:
(Insert photo or draw image that connects to memory)

Why are you grateful for this story?
(lesson learned, how you felt, long term impact)

_____

_____

_____

_____

_____

_____

_____

_____

(Insert word here)

Context Clues

1) _____

2) _____

3) _____

_____
(Name your story)

Life Stage: _____
(Child, Teen, Adult, etc.)

Place: _____

Characters:

Memory Box:
(Insert photo or draw image that connects to memory)

Why are you grateful for this story?
(lesson learned, how you felt, long term impact)

_____

_____

_____

_____

_____

_____

_____

_____

Context Clues

1) _____
2) _____
3) _____

(Insert word here)

_____
(Name your story)

Life Stage: _____   **Place:** _____
(Child, Teen, Adult, etc.)

Characters:

Memory Box:
(Insert photo or draw image that connects to memory)

Why are you grateful for this story?
(lesson learned, how you felt, long term impact)

(Insert word here)

Context Clues

1) ....

2) ....

3) ....

_____

(Name your story)

Life Stage: _____   Place: _____
(Child, Teen, Adult, etc.)

Characters:

Memory Box:
(Insert photo or draw image that connects to memory)

Why are you grateful for this story?
(lesson learned, how you felt, long term impact)

_____

_____

_____

_____

_____

_____

_____

_____

Context Clues

1) _____
2) _____
3) _____

[ ]

(Insert word here)

_____
(Name your story)

_____

_____

_____

_____

_____

_____

_____

_____

_____

_____

_____

_____

_____

_____

_____

_____

_____

_____

_____

_____

_____

Life Stage: _____

(Child, Teen, Adult, etc.)

Place: _____

Characters:

Memory Box:

(Insert photo or draw image that connects to memory)

Why are you grateful for this story?

(lesson learned, how you felt, long term impact)

(Insert word here)

Context Clues

1) _____
2) _____
3) _____

(Name your story)

_____

_____

_____

_____

_____

_____

_____

_____

_____

_____

_____

_____

_____

_____

_____

_____

_____

_____

_____

_____

_____

Life Stage: _____
(Child, Teen, Adult, etc.)

Place: _____

Characters:

Memory Box:
(Insert photo or draw image that connects to memory)

Why are you grateful for this story?
(lesson learned, how you felt, long term impact)

_____

_____

_____

_____

_____

_____

_____

_____

Context Clues

1) _____

2) _____

3) _____

(Insert word here)

_____
(Name your story)

Life Stage: _____

(Child, Teen, Adult, etc.)

Place: _____

Characters:

Memory Box:

(Insert photo or draw image that connects to memory)

Why are you grateful for this story?

(lesson learned, how you felt, long term impact)

_____

_____

_____

_____

_____

_____

_____

(Insert word here)

Context Clues

1) _____
2) _____
3) _____

_____
(Name your story)

Life Stage: _____   **Place:** _____
(Child, Teen, Adult, etc.)

Characters:

Memory Box:
(Insert photo or draw image that connects to memory)

Why are you grateful for this story?
(lesson learned, how you felt, long term impact)

_____
_____
_____
_____
_____
_____
_____
_____

(Insert word here)

Context Clues
1) _____
2) _____
3) _____

_____
(Name your story)

_____
_____
_____
_____
_____
_____
_____
_____
_____
_____
_____
_____
_____
_____
_____
_____
_____
_____
_____
_____
_____

Life Stage: _____   **Place:** _____
(Child, Teen, Adult, etc.)

Characters:

Memory Box:
(Insert photo or draw image that connects to memory)

Why are you grateful for this story?
(lesson learned, how you felt, long term impact)

_____

_____

_____

_____

_____

_____

_____

(Insert word here)

Context Clues

1) _____

2) _____

3) _____

_____
(Name your story)

Life Stage: _____   **Place:** _____
(Child, Teen, Adult, etc.)

Characters:

Memory Box:
(Insert photo or draw image that connects to memory)

Why are you grateful for this story?
(lesson learned, how you felt, long term impact)

_____

_____

_____

_____

_____

_____

_____

Context Clues

1) _____
2) _____
3) _____

(Insert word here)

_____
(Name your story)

Life Stage: _____

(Child, Teen, Adult, etc.)

Place: _____

Characters:

Memory Box:
(Insert photo or draw image that connects to memory)

Why are you grateful for this story?
(lesson learned, how you felt, long term impact)

_____

_____

_____

_____

_____

_____

_____

(Insert word here)

Context Clues

1) _____
2) _____
3) _____

_____
(Name your story)

Life Stage: _____ **Place:** _____
(Child, Teen, Adult, etc.)

Characters:

Memory Box:
(Insert photo or draw image that connects to memory)

Why are you grateful for this story?
(lesson learned, how you felt, long term impact)

_____

_____

_____

_____

_____

_____

_____

_____

Context Clues

(Insert word here)

1) _____
2) _____
3) _____

_____
(Name your story)

Life Stage: _____   **Place:** _____
(Child, Teen, Adult, etc.)

Characters:

Memory Box:
(Insert photo or draw image that connects to memory)

Why are you grateful for this story?
(lesson learned, how you felt, long term impact)

(Insert word here)

Context Clues

1) _____
2) _____
3) _____

_____
(Name your story)

Life Stage: _____   **Place:** _____
(Child, Teen, Adult, etc.)

Characters:

Memory Box:
(Insert photo or draw image that connects to memory)

Why are you grateful for this story?
(lesson learned, how you felt, long term impact)

_____

_____

_____

_____

_____

_____

_____

_____

Context Clues

1) _____

2) _____

3) _____

(Insert word here)

_____
(Name your story)

_____

_____

_____

_____

_____

_____

_____

_____

_____

_____

_____

_____

_____

_____

_____

_____

_____

_____

_____

Life Stage: _____
(Child, Teen, Adult, etc.)

Place: _____

Characters:

Memory Box:
(Insert photo or draw image that connects to memory)

Why are you grateful for this story?
(lesson learned, how you felt, long term impact)

_____
_____
_____
_____
_____
_____
_____
_____

(Insert word here)

Context Clues

1) _____

2) _____

3) _____

(Name your story)

Life Stage: _____ **Place:** _____
(Child, Teen, Adult, etc.)

Characters:

Memory Box:
(Insert photo or draw image that connects to memory)

Why are you grateful for this story?
(lesson learned, how you felt, long term impact)

_____
_____
_____
_____
_____
_____
_____
_____